We Smile

COMMUNICATION & COOPERATION STRATEGIES FOR HEALING, INTIMACY, & TEAMWORK

Bonnie L. Bair, LCPC

Life Improvements

Galesburg, Illinois

Names: Bair, Bonnie L. | Bair, Todd M. editor

Title: We Smile | by Bonnie L. Bair, LCPC

Description: 1st edition. | Galesburg; Illinois: Life Improvements, 2017

Subject: Communication & Cooperation Strategies for Healing, Intimacy, & Teamwork

Identifiers: LCCN 2017915664 print | e(book)

IBSN 978-0-9994772-1-2 paperback | ISBN 978-0-9994772-0-5 e(book)

Dedicated to God and Humanity

Table of Contents

Special Thanks To:

-My God and His Holy Spirit.

-My Lord and Savior, Jesus Christ.

-My Parents, for their sacrifices, love and commitment to each other for over 55 years.

-My Husband, for his sacrifice, love, and faithfulness for over 25 years.

-My Daughter, for challenging me and motivating me to grow and learn.

-My Sister, for her years of encouragement.

-My Clients, for sharing their experiences with me.

-Other family, friends, teachers, pastors, health professionals, students, neighbors and strangers; for teaching me about life and relationships.

-My Readers ☺

Introduction

Relationships are the key to our existence. The better they are, the better we feel. Studying relationships for 33 years, being a marriage counselor for 10 years and being married for 25 years, has helped me write this book. My hope is to help others to more fully enjoy life & relationships.

Our Self   Chapter I

The first step for enjoying healthy happy relationships, is to look at the self. The quality of our relationships, are contingent on our willingness to assess and address our own attitudes, behaviors and beliefs. The more willing we are to assess and make minor changes, the more likely we are to enjoy more satisfying relationships. Mutual respect and equality in relationships require each person to do their own part in creating win/win situations and solutions.

Our Mind and Affirmations

Affirmations can help us make behavior change easier. Using affirmations, is a simple and effective technique that incorporates the help of the sub-conscious mind. Affirmations can help us reach our individual and relationship goals. They can be used in combination with prayer and visualization.

I learned about affirmations from a conference done by Brian Tracy, PHD. The concept of affirmations sounded too good to be true, to me, at the time. However, I was having troubles being on time for work. I had not been able to change my behavior on my own, so I decided to give it a try. What did I have to lose?

Therefore, I began stating "I am early or on time for all appointments" over and over for 1-2 minutes a day, as Mr. Tracy suggested. I often thought, "This is stupid. I'm just lying to myself." I further thought, I will just keep saying it to see if it really works. Nothing else has worked thus far. What do I have to lose?"

About 10 days into saying, "I am early or on time for all appointments," I got to work and looked at the clock. The time on the clock was 6:50 am. I was bewildered and stated the clock must be wrong. My co-worker looked at me as if I was crazy and said it was the correct time. I proceeded to go and look at the clock in the other room. It also read 6:50 am. At that point, I was in major disbelief. I remember exclaiming "How can that be?" "I did not hurry to work!" "I got here without rushing, for once in my life, and I am early!" "How did that happen?" Then I remembered: I had been saying the affirmations.

Since then, I have regularly used affirmations to change behavior and reach my goals. It can be very powerful to do so. I have encouraged my clients to do likewise. Louise Hay is an author who has written affirmations for specific illnesses to use to help heal the body. Her book is titled, <u>You Can Heal Your Life</u>.

Common behaviors that cause problems in relationships can be helped with these affirmations:

To quit smoking: *"My lungs are clearing."*

To stop drinking alcohol: *"I drink plenty of water."*

To stop procrastinating: *"I just do it. I'm responsible!*

To complete tasks: *"I stay focused and finish what I start!"*

To keep from beating up self after making a mistake: *"That was then. This is now!"*

To lessen anxiety: *"I pray, smile and relax!" "I know what to do!"*

To help couples: *"We work together as a team and find win/win solutions!"*

To share feelings: *"I say how I feel and what I need with ease!"*

To overcome depression: *"I'm feeling better."*

To feel better about self: *"I like myself more each day."*

To be able to say, "No to others, when needed: *"I say No with love and ease."*

To forgive myself and others: *"I forgive, and I let go." "That was then. This is now!"*

Affirmations work when said out loud repeatedly, (1-2 minutes/day) because the sub-conscious mind is awake all the time. The sub-conscious follows what you say with your mouth. It helps you solve problems and reach goals. As you adjust what you think and say, the changes you desire begin to happen. Thoughts such as, "This isn't true." "This is stupid. I am lying to myself." will probably come to mind. Just ignore and continue to aim for your target.

For anyone concerned about this technique being based in psychology and not the word of God, let me put your mind at ease. These scriptures line up with this very practice.

Be careful what you think, for your thoughts run your life. Proverbs 4:23

Take every thought captive. 2 Cor. 10:4-5 **As a man thinks in his heart, so he is.** Proverbs 23:7

Do not doubt. Instead, believe those things you say will be done and you will have whatever you say. Mark 11:23 (Jesus' said this at least 3 times in the gospels)

Not only can affirmations be effective, it is also important to keep your speech in line with what you are hoping for. If a person has been having difficulty getting pregnant, they will want to speak as though the difficulty has been in the past. For example: "I've been having difficulty getting pregnant. When I get pregnant ......" lines up with the goal. Whereas: "I can't get pregnant or If, I get pregnant..." does not line up with the goal. *The sub-conscious mind hears what we say.* If we want our mind to help us get there, we need to consciously put it on notice and give it the direction we want it to have.

The life affirmation I have written below, helps me stay on track with my own attitudes, goals, and behavior related to health and happiness in life and relationships. If you like it, use it.

My Daily Affirmation

I just do it! I'm responsible! And God is on my side! ☺

I ask for help when I need it. And I thankfully receive it!

I work hard. I use my mind. I am curious and kind!

I listen with my heart. And gladly do my part!

I say sorry for my mistakes; and forgiveness I do take!

I acknowledge my own needs. And I care for my body!

I pray, smile and relax, so I achieve the max!

I say the truth. I show respect. Limitations I accept!

That was then, and this is now! What to do, I seek and how!

As I do my best, I trust God to do the rest!

I choose love and I let go! What to do, this I do know!

Satan cannot take me! And God, He did create me!

I enjoy being me! Because of Jesus, I am free!

I count my blessings! And because of all these things; I dance and sing!

I just do it! I'm responsible! And God is on my side! ☺

Our Body

How we care for our bodies also affect our lives and relationships. The quality of food or nutrients and medicine we take, sleep, and the exercise we get; all help determine the quality and length of life we spend with those we love.

Health Issues that Affect Our Bodies/Relationships

1. Inadequate sleep

We all know how important sleep is to our bodies. According to the Koala Center for Sleep, inadequate sleep can lead to depression and anxiety. Sleep apnea and TMJ issues affect quality of sleep. If you suspect either one, it's worth it to get treated. Seek out professional help as necessary. Many of my clients have benefited by taking 250 mg of magnesium, prior to bed time since it can help relax the nerves. Others have noticed improvement with sleep when they have taken 2.5-5 mg of chewable melatonin. Others benefit from taking both magnesium and melatonin together. There are other treatment options for poor sleep. If sleep is an issue, please do your research and discuss with your doctor, as it affects your health/relationships.

Affirmations that can help with sleeping are:

To sleep better: *"I sleep like a rock!"*

To stop mind from racing when trying to sleep: *"I stop thinking and start sleeping!"*

2. Inadequate Magnesium Intake

Not only can magnesium help with sleep, it can help also prevent depression, anxiety, migraine headaches, acid reflux, and muscles cramps. Often, clients report feeling happier and less anxious after a week of taking 250 mg of magnesium supplementation.

3. Inadequate Vitamin D Intake

Inadequate supplies of Vitamin D, especially in the winter months, can contribute to depression. I often suggest to clients with seasonal affective disorder (who are depressed in the winter months) to take Vitamin D once the time changes in the fall until the time changes again in the spring. In the winter months, some of us do not get adequate doses of sunlight for our body to produce enough Vitamin D on its own.

4.   Inadequate Breakdown of Folic Acid

I learned from Dr. Matthew Preston, that some families do not carry the gene that adequately breaks down folic acid. L-methyl folate is a more elemental form of folic acid that can be used easily by the body. It may take the body weeks or months of supplementation with l-methyl folate to reverse depression or anxiety caused by inadequate utilization of folic acid.

5. Anxiety

Caffeine and artificial sweeteners can contribute to anxiety. Reducing intake of both should help reduce anxiety. ***Doing a Kegel exercise with any worry thoughts can help reduce anxiety significantly over time.*** According to a conference I attended by J. Eric Gentry, Ph.D., a Kegel exercise will help to reset the Vagus nerve (The main nerve that runs from our brain to our pelvis) and will send peaceful signals to the body; rather than stress signals. It causes the body to breathe deeper. It also helps the brain map new pathways for dealing with stress. The body cannot hold a peaceful and a stress response at the same time. It's one or the other.

Remember, anxiety is a signal to the body to do something. It usually requires you to do something; talk to someone, ask for help or take some other action. When something is totally out of our control; we can pray, do a Kegel, take a deep breath and let it go or forget about it.

As stated earlier, inadequate processing of folic acid, low levels of magnesium and inadequate sleep, can all contribute to anxiety. Often, clients report less panic, when supplementing with magnesium. Holy Basil (400-800 mg) seems to help Social Anxiety. Do your research and ask.

6. Depression

Magnesium is often also helpful in treating depression. Clients generally report noticing improvement in mood after a week of supplementation with magnesium.

Some clients with anxiety and depression report noticeable reduction of symptoms when they take St John's Wart. (It's important to note that St. John's Wart should not be taken with any other anti-depressants nor should it be taken by anyone with Bi-polar I disorder.)

There are various medical factors that can contribute to depression and irritability: inadequate sleep, low magnesium levels, low hormone levels, inadequate processing of folic acid, low levels of vitamin D, etc.

Moderate to severe depression is no laughing matter and needs attention. Consultation with medical professionals for testing and treatment options can make life much more manageable.

7. Diabetes/Hypoglycemia

Blood sugar issues can cause irritability and mood swings. Monitoring blood sugar levels is essential for stabilization and management.

8. Drug or Alcohol Usage

Substance use and abuse can contribute to mental health issues. Or, in many cases, individuals use drugs or alcohol to self- medicates an undiagnosed mental health condition such as anxiety, depression, bi-polar disorder, etc. There is medicine available to help people stop using drugs and drinking. One can ask a medical doctor or psychiatrist for help - if this is the case.

9. Gluten Intolerance

Gluten is a protein found in wheat and other grains. Individuals with the gluten intolerant gene may have anxiety, depression, acid reflux, migraine, or bi-polar type symptoms. Genetic testing can be done to identify gluten intolerance. However, a person, who is gluten sensitive, usually improves once they avoid gluten.

10. Bi-Polar Disorder

Anxiety and depression are present in bi-polar disorder. ***Medications having mood stabilizing properties are essential for treating bi-polar disorder.*** Bipolar 1 disorder is different from Bi-polar 2 disorder. <u>Regular anti-depressants, without any mood stabilizing properties, can make bi-polar disorder (especially bi-polar 1 disorder) worse.</u> Also, Estrogen (or the birth control pill) can interfere with Bi-polar medication; making it less effective in treating bi-polar disorder. I have seen some individuals have success managing bi-polar disorder with a combination of CBD oil and Ashwaganda (400-800 mg). The CBD oil helps stabilize mood and help reduce anger. Ashwaganda can help a person focus and handle stress better. It has helped individuals I know, be more aware of time and thus more punctual. I will speak about bi-polar disorder more in the following chapter.

Regardless of the medical issue, it is important to take responsibility, do your research and check with medical health professionals to accurately pin-point and treat medical issues affecting both your body and your relationships.

Please note: Psychiatrists have four additional years of medical training directly related to the brain/medicines than general physicians do.

Bi-Polar Disorder and How to Cope/Deal with it

Having bi-polar disorder is not a sin or something to be ashamed of. Bi-polar disorder is usually always inherited. There is some research that shows head injury can contribute to bi-polar disorder. It is often misunderstood, undiagnosed and inadequately treated.

First, what is Bi-Polar Disorder?

People with bi-polar disorder tend to be very creative, compassionate, and intelligent. Individuals with bi-polar disorder often have difficulty with distraction, racing thoughts, memory, anxiety, ADD or ADHA type symptoms, and can have sudden changes in mood/behavior/sleep patterns/energy level. Early indicators of the disease can be: uncomfortable clothing or tags in the back of shirts being problematic.

Individuals with bi-polar disorder may exhibit 1 or more of the following:

1. Drug or Alcohol Addiction: Persons with bi-polar disorder often unknowingly self-medicate through alcohol or drugs. During a manic cycle (when things get overwhelming and out of control) they may sub-consciously use alcohol or marijuana to level themselves off, so they can cope with things better. During a depressed cycle, they may use drugs or alcohol to help them not care about things so much. Without medication, they need drugs or alcohol for stabilization and survival.

2. Spending sprees or gambling problems
3. Suicide attempts or suicidal thoughts (can indicate bi-polar 2 disorder)
4. High Irritability
5. Inappropriate or many sexual relationships
6. Extreme religious experiences or work-a-holism may even be an indicator for some individuals

It is important to see a psychiatrist for accurate diagnoses and treatment if bi-polar disorder is suspected, especially if another family member has bi-polar disorder.
Improper or inadequate treatment of bi-polar disorder can be dangerous. I have found regular medical doctors do not always know how to treat bi-polar disorder accurately. Sometimes they may treat it with a regular anti-depressant, which can make things worse. Accurate communication of the symptoms and asking questions about medications with mood stabilizing properties will help regular physicians and psychiatrists to select the best medication for yourself

or your loved one. Often it is necessary to try more than one medication or a different dosage of medication, to successfully manage bi-polar symptoms.

Each person is different and may respond differently to medications. It's essential to communicate and follow-up closely with the medical provider; especially when a person is not feeling well on a certain medication. Stopping the medication without medical supervision can make things worse and will not give the professional the opportunity to provide the individual with another medical solution. Bi-polar disorder usually always requires medication or some nutrient to support the body. There is a chemical imbalance that needs to be addressed. Bi-polar symptoms tend to get worse with age and stress situations. It's important to have medication in a person's system, so they can handle stressors when they happen. There is some research regarding nutritional alternatives to medicine for treating bi-polar disorder. Often, individuals with bi-polar disorder are very against taking any medicine for it. However, it does need treatment in some way, for the person to function at their best for living and having happy relationships. It's important to do extensive research/or check with the professionals before treating bi-polar disorder. The kind of treatment will depend on the type of bi-polar disorder it is. Bi-polar disorder often shows up during a person's early to mid- twenties.

How to Manage Bi-polar Disorder

It is very important for individuals with bi-polar disorder to get adequate regular sleep (7-10 hours per night), eat healthy foods at regular intervals (skipping meals can trigger mania in some individuals), have a moderate exercise routine, have daily quiet time to themselves, slow down and keep the number of activities and expectations to a minimum - especially during times of stress, take daily nutrients/medication (until a cure is discovered), and practice routines with variety to prevent boredom. An example of this is to eat at the same approximate time each day and vary what you eat, where you eat, or who you eat with. Individuals with bi-polar disorder tend to become bored very easily. It's very helpful to plan for boredom, ahead of time.

Often individuals with bi-polar disorder may feel judged by others and feel more inadequate, overwhelmed, frustrated, and angry when others don't understand.

Family and Friends of individuals with bi-polar disorder might feel inadequate and scared because they don't know how to help or what to do. Remember, you can simply let the other person know you care and ask them how you can help. Be willing to do something for them in exchange for them getting help and taking their medicine or nutrients (such as the combination of CBD oil and Ashwaganda 400-800 mg), can be helpful. It is also often helpful for someone to accompany them to doctor appointments, for complete information sharing with health providers for adequate medicine management. Education and an atmosphere of understanding, love and acceptance, will help the most. According to the National Institute of Mental Health, "Bi-polar disorder affects approximately 5.7 million adult Americans, or about 2.6% of the U.S. population age 18 and older, every year."

For Parents with children with ADD and Bi-polar disorder: It's important to remember to <u>slow life down and make 1 request at a time</u> (because of high distraction and feelings of overwhelm). *It may help to gently touch them on the shoulder or back when you make the request, in a loving tone, to get their attention and cooperation.* Cut out excess stimuli. Keep things simple and keep requests limited to 1-3 tasks per day (yet keep standards). Their ability may vary from day to day. One day they may be able to do a lot and function well. Yet the next day they may not be able to function hardly at all. ***Remember, they will need down time for themselves each day.*** This will help keep frustration, anger, and disrespectful behavior at bay.

Our Emotions

Dealing with Our Own Emotions

I have found that it is common for people to have difficulty in dealing with emotions, be it our own or others. Mental health issues can complicate matters further. That's why it is so important to be as healthy as possible. Anxiety and depression can increase when we do not know how to deal with our own emotions, or the emotions of others.

Following, I have listed some healthy responses we might have to various emotions of our own and of other people. Knowing and practicing our options ahead of time can help us deal with our own emotions and respond more appropriately to other's emotions.

Examples of Healthy thoughts we can Think/Say when WE are feeling:

Crabby   Think: This won't last forever. Am I hungry, tired, or do I need something?

Say: *"I'm sorry I've been crabby. I've been feeling hungry. I need to eat."*

Overwhelmed   Think: I can handle this. I can start with the easiest task or ask for help.

Say: *"I'm feeling overwhelmed. Would you mind helping me?"*

Condemned/Judged   Think: I am human and so are they.

Say: *"Judge not, that you be not judged"*. Or, "*Will you forgive me?"*

Accused/Blamed   Think: I am responsible for my actions or both of us are at fault.

Say: **"I am sorry and** *am taking responsibility for my part in this. Will you do the same?"*

Angry   Think: What am I angry about? What do I need? What will make it better?

Say: *"I'm angry about ____? I need ____? Would you be willing to ____?"*

Interrupted Think: They must be forgetful or unaware that I'm busy.

Say: *"Would you mind if I finish this? Then I can give you my full attention."*

Guilty   Think: I can ask for forgiveness.

Say: *"I'm sorry. Will you forgive me?"*

Betrayed   Think: <u>What caused them to do what they did?</u>

Say: *"I feel betrayed. Would you be willing to explain?"*

Ashamed   Think: <u>I acknowledge my actions/behavior and take responsibility.</u>

Say: *"I feel ashamed and regret my behavior or attitude."*

Worried   Think: <u>What do I need to do? I can figure this out.</u>

Say: *"I'm feeling concerned about _____?"*

Ignored   Think: <u>They must have a lot on their mind or be busy. Maybe they do not know what to do or say.</u>

Say: *"Hey, would you be willing to give me some attention?"* Or, *"When is a good time for us to talk or spend some time together?"*

Unworthy   Think: <u>I am human. God loves me, anyway.</u>

Say: *"I've been feeling unworthy. Thank you for _____."*

Unappreciated   Think: <u>Even though they haven't said thank you, they probably do appreciate it. I can ask them if they appreciated what I did.</u>

Ask, *"Did you appreciate what I did for you?"*

Inadequate/Stupid   Think: <u>I am doing my best and am capable of learning and willing to like myself.</u>

Say: *"I'm feeling inadequate or ignorant at this moment."*

Sad/Hurt   Think: <u>I feel sad or hurt at this moment. It will not last forever. I can ask for an apology, if I want to. Or I can do something that will help me feel better.</u>

Say: *"I have been feeling sad."*

Bitter/Resentful   Think: <u>That was then. And this is now.</u> Say: *"I forgive and let it go!"*

Examples of What to Say/Do when OTHERS are feeling:

Crabby *"Is there something you need?"*

Overwhelmed *"How can I help?"*

Sick *"Can I get or do anything for you?"*

Condemned *"I cannot judge you."*

Accused/Blamed *"I take responsibility for my part in the matter."*

Angry *"I don't blame you. I understand."* Or, *"Is there something you need?"*

Worried *"Can I do something to help or would you like me to pray with or for you?"*

Interrupted *"Excuse me, please? I'm sorry to interrupt."*

Guilty *"I forgive you!"*

Betrayed *"I understand."*

Ashamed *"No Worries! We all make mistakes!"*

Ignored *"How are you today? What's going on?"*

Unworthy *"We are all human."*

Unappreciated *"I really appreciate what you did for me."* And give a gift or a hug.

Inadequate/Stupid *"I understand. I have felt that way before."*

Sad/Hurt *"I'm sorry I hurt you." "How can I make it up to you?"* Or, *"I'm sorry you are hurting."*

Bitter/Resentful *"I'm sorry you were hurt."*

Our Spirit

Our Spirit plays a role in affecting our mind, body, emotions, and relationships. Just as we need adequate food, sleep and exercise to maintain our body, we also need to tend to our spiritual needs. Practicing these seven spiritual practices, will positively affect our relationships/lives.

1. **Being thankful helps our relationships with God and others and causes us peace.**

    Let the peace of God rule in your hearts, to which you were called in one body, and become thankful. **Colossians 3:15**

2. **Listening helps us gain understanding, builds relationships, and causes happiness.**

    Everyone must be quick to hear, slow to speak and slow to anger. **James 1:19**
    Happy is the person who finds wisdom and gains understanding. **Proverbs 3:13**

3. **Giving to others helps not only others, but also helps ourselves.**

    Give and it shall be given unto you. **Luke 6:38**

4. **Going to God when we need something helps us and our relationships. God wants to help us with our everyday life issues and concerns.**

    In every situation, by prayer and petition (with thanksgiving), present your requests to God. And the peace of God will be with you. **Philippians 4:6-7**

5. **Seeking God daily, helps us to love others and be blessed ourselves. Reading God's word helps us to hear and follow accurately.**

    Blessed is the person who listens to me (God), watching daily at my doors, waiting at my door-way. For those who find me, find life. Those who fail to find me, harm themselves. **Proverbs 8:34-36.**

    A day that begins and ends in prayer, won't become unraveled. **Psalm 92:1-2**

6. Making sure we have a day to rest each week, allows rejuvenation in our body and spirit. It helps us to be at our best for others.

    Remember the Sabbath Day to keep it holy. Six days you should labor and do all your work; but, the seventh day is the Sabbath of the Lord (**Exodus 20:8**), *and you should rest.*

7. Listening to God's word builds our faith for healing and miracles. God wants to do the impossible in our lives.

    Faith comes by hearing the word of God. **Romans 10:17**

    Faith is the substance of things hoped for, the evidence of things not seen. **Hebrews 11:1**

Understanding Differences and Overcoming Difficulties

Biological Differences in Men and Women Affecting Relationships

1) Physical Connections is to Men as Emotional Connection is to Women

I think I first heard it from Gary Smalley that women connect emotionally, and men connect physically. Usually men need physical connection to feel safe and want to connect emotionally. Women need the emotional connection to want to connect physically. It takes both people to move out of their comfort zones and choose to love the other person in the way the other needs to be loved. Taking turns is a wonderful solution.

2) Men are at a disadvantage in winning arguments with women.

Men use only one side of their brain in communication, while women use both sides of their brain. This makes women's stories and emotions hard to follow. Because of this, women often misunderstand and think men don't care. This contributes to hostility from women and avoidance by men.

It typically takes a man longer to process and respond appropriately, due to having 6.5 times more "gray matter" (thinking matter) in the brain. Women have more 9.5 times more "white matter" in the brain. It connects parts of the brain together and allows women to respond and communicate more quickly. *Therefore, it helps if women are more direct with communication and give men time to respond to one thing before bringing up another.*

*It's important to know how men and women brains are designed for getting along better.

Women have fewer red blood cells and therefore, tire more easily. They are more emotionally responsive and therefore, laugh and cry more easily. Women are more verbal and relational than men and tend to be kinder and more people oriented. Therefore, they will care about who is involved and will enjoy solving problems together more than men will. Women are usually better at multi-tasking and are global thinkers. This can cause them to be more prone to becoming overwhelmed. Women revisit emotional memories and analyze. They are faster and more accurate at identifying emotions. Because women feel closer and more validated through dialogue, they can get frustrated easily when their male counterpart is not as communicative with them.

On the other hand, men have more blood and muscles than women, which makes men typically stronger than their women counterparts. They are less sensitive to the cold and have a larger brain and thicker skull. They think about and seek sex more than women do. Sex is how men express their softer side. Men tend to be more focused and have better follow through because of it. They often keep problems to themselves and like to solve problems alone. Men tend to be linear thinkers and can separate themselves from problems. They reflect more briefly on emotions and because of it, may frustrate their female counterparts when they don't want to discuss things at length.

Men and women approach problems with similar goals, but with different considerations. Problems arise when we expect the opposite sex to think, feel, or act the way we do. As we understand and accept our differences, we will be less frustrating to each other. We will compromise and get along better.

There are some exceptions to the above male/female differences. In some cases, certain things may be reversed in some couples. Usually the main differences exist in every couple, due to opposites attracting. Being aware of the differences are helpful.

The above sources, for the information on the biological differences between Men and Women, are the following: Gary Smalley, Michael Conner, Web M.D., Psychology Today, Lawrence Wilson, MD, Athena Health, and Dr. James Dobson.

Social Differences in Men and Women Affecting Relationships

Over the years in working with couples, *I have found that men often feel it is their job to please their spouse. Because of this, they tend to avoid sharing things that might be upsetting; especially those things that make their spouse cry.* Their lack of sharing can be offensive to the women they live with. Then they can feel more inadequate when their spouse is more upset. They are known to say things like: "Don't worry about it!" This minimizing of concerns their spouse may have, can come across to their spouse as if they don't care; which is usually quite the opposite of what is happening. It's because men do care and don't want their wives to be upset.

Similarly, women have been socialized to please the men in their lives. Because of this, they tend to give beyond what they are comfortable. In doing this, resentment can build. They can become very unhappy and sometimes unwilling to continue with the relationship.

Men are programmed that it's their job to provide for their spouse and to fix things. This often can result in men putting their needs aside for so long that it builds resentment and then they are more irritable and difficult to live with. Or it can result in men trying to fix a problem without acknowledging their wife's feeling to their wife. *Since feelings are so important to women, it's important to women that the men they live with acknowledge and understand their feelings.*

Conversely, women can make men uncomfortable when talking about feelings. As we learned earlier, men are not as good at identifying feelings or communicating. The difference is magnified because historically, girls practice talking about and identifying feelings; while boys are often taught to shake things off- so to speak. It makes the disparity between men and women greater and can make getting along more difficult.

Relationship Difficulties

Another societal contributor to difficulty in relationships is dirty fighting. Unfortunately, we have all learned unhealthy ways of interacting with others and of getting what we want - some of us more than others.

How to Stop Unhealthy Reactions/Interactions

Approximately 26 years ago, I attended a class created by Paul Hegstrom and taught by Dixie Carter. The class was called Learning to Live - Learning to Love. It was a class created to reduce domestic violence and help heal individuals from all kinds of abuse; including emotional, physical and spiritual abuse. I learned many things in the 12-week course. One of the most valuable pieces of information included Dirty Fighting Techniques. Little did I know, but I was a habitual user of several of them. I soon realized it is common for all of us to have habits we are unaware of. Once the awareness comes, behavior can be changes. What an eye-opening experience it was for me!

We all learn undesired ways of interacting that can make situations worse and more complicated, instead of better. Awareness is the key. Until one is aware of what they are doing and knows how to change it, they probably will continue the destructive behavior.

The following is a list of common fighting scenarios. The ideas/affirmations, on how to respond and how to stop or change destructive behavior, follow.

When couples use specific affirmations to reprogram their sub-conscious for responding to another person's problem behavior and for addressing their own problem behavior, the frequency and intensity of fighting lessens immensely.

Step 1 **Awareness** – usually produces humility and leads to forgiveness.

Step 2 **Knowing** how to de-escalate and prevent future fighting.

Step 3 **Changing** your own behavior to get the desired result.

What to do when someone avoids: *Tell them you would like to discuss subject_____. Ask them when a good time would be for them to be willing to discuss _____ with you.*

What to do when someone blames: **First, acknowledge and take responsibility for your own behavior and how it contributed to the problem. Second, kindly ask the other person to acknowledge what aspect of their behavior contributed to the problem.**

How to Stop Unhealthy Reactions/Interactions Continued

<u>What to do when someone bullies you:</u> **Ask them if they can think of a way in which both of you can get something you both want.**

Affirmation to stop bullying: *We create win/win solutions!"*

<u>What to do when someone complains of more than one thing at a time?</u> *Tell the other person you feel overwhelmed and need to discuss one issue at a time, so you can properly address their concerns.*

Affirmation: *"We discuss one issue at a time (when it happens), at our established talk time.* Also, *"That was then, this is now!"* will help stick to the present issue.

<u>What to do when someone demands answers.</u> *Acknowledge the other person's disappointment, first. Second, you may ask the other person to tell you how they are feeling.*

Affirmation to stop demands: *"I realize things will not always turnout the ways I expect them to."* Instead of using the word *"why,"* try stating, *"I am wondering what happened that you were later than expected."*

<u>What to do when someone is frustrated with you?</u> **Acknowledge the other person's feelings of frustration. Be willing to and tell the other person your willingness to make efforts to adjust your behavior in the future.**

<u>What to do when someone says they are going to do something equally as wrong, because you did something.</u> **First, acknowledge past hurtful behavior of your own. Second, ask the other person to take responsibility for their own actions, as well.**

<u>What to do when someone leaves:</u> **Wait a while. When they return, ask them if they are ready to discuss the issue. If they are not, acknowledge feelings of hesitation or fear in addressing the issue. Ask them when they might be willing to discuss it or if they think it would be better to discuss via writing.**

Affirmation to stop leaving: *"If I need time to calm down or to think, I can ask for twenty minutes to collect my thoughts and tell the other person I will be ready to discuss it then. I can write down my thoughts to the other person, if I think it will help one or both of us." If I need a longer time to process or calm down, I can ask the other person for it and tell them when I think I might be able to discuss the subject."* This will lessen anxiety.

How to Stop Unhealthy Reactions/Interactions Continued

What to do when someone calls you a name: **Acknowledge your own feelings of disrespect and ask the person to tell you how they are feeling, in a respectful way.**

What to do when a person says, "You will never change:" **Acknowledge the other person's feelings and address concerns. Request the other person to express their concerns and expect you to do your best to find mutually agreeable solutions in the future.**

When a person is sarcastic and then implies something is wrong with you for how you heard a complaint: **Tell the other person what you think they might be thinking and how they might be feeling. Ask them if you are correct. Secondly, you can simply ask the person to tell you how they feel in the future and assure them you care about them and their needs.**

When someone implies there should be a break up: **First, acknowledge the other person's frustration/needs, as well as your own. Remember, everyone is can change. You can ask the other person if they would be willing to do what is needed, in exchange for something else.**

When a person starts an argument at a bad time: **Remember to have or ask for discussions with others at times that work for both people. Tell the person you would like to discuss the issue at a better time. Suggest an alternative time to discuss the matter. This will help reduce anxiety for both people.**

What to do when a person implies they are better than the other for some reason? **Agree with any true statements the other person makes and remind the other person that your view, needs, and contributions are important too. Then ask the other person to find a win/win solution, in which both of you are 80% satisfied.**

When someone ignores the other: **Remember, if it's not a good time for you or the other person to listen, arrangements can be made for another specific time to listen to or discuss a topic. Do your best to approach each other in ways and at times that are convenient for both of you.**

When someone is holding a grudge: **Ask or tell what can be done to help with forgiveness. Remind each other: That was then. This is now!**

How to Stop Unhealthy Reactions/Interactions Continued

When someone is compared to someone else they don't like or are angry with: **"Acknowledge there may be some similarities and acknowledge the other persons frustration and/or anxiety. Also, Take responsibility for your own attitudes and behavior.** *Affirm: "I would not like to be compared in negative ways to others. Therefore, I will not do it to anyone else."*

What to do when words like "always," "every," "all," and "never" are used in an argument: **Instead use words like "often," "seldom," "sometimes," "rarely," etc. "This helps other people to respond productively when there is no exaggeration.**

Note: Using the word "BUT" negates what a person said prior to the word "but".

Silly example: "I love you, but you drive me crazy!" **(Versus)** "I love you & you drive me crazy!"

Affirm: "Others will listen to me much better when I use the word "AND."

*The above list of unhealthy interactions was derived from a dirty fighting list from Paul Hegstrom's work at Life Skills International. The affirmations and responses to stop unhealthy reactions/Interactions are my own. Another unhealthy interaction is the use of guilt.

When a person tries to make another feel guilty: This is usually done when the person wants acknowledgement, an apology a thank you, or maybe even cooperation. **Ask the other person what the guilt is about and what it is they need.** They probably don't realize they are using guilt.

Another source of contention is when different words have different meanings to different people. For example: Within the first 4 years of being married, my husband and I got into some arguments over number words. Upon further questioning, I realized we had different meanings for the same words. He learned somewhere that the word "few" meant 2-3. And the word "several" meant 3-4. Whereas, I learned the word "few" meant 4-5 and "several" meant 6-8. This difference can be confusing and important when discussing a "few" hundred or "several hundred" dollars – if you know what I mean. When something doesn't sound right, remember to check out the other person's frame of reference.

General Affirmations for Healthy Interactions

"I take responsibility for my own feelings, attitudes, and behaviors."

"I think the best of others and treat them with the respect I would want to be treated with."

If someone does or says something I don't like, I can ask them to simply tell me why they are upset. I then ask what they need.

"I acknowledge and discuss concerns with others." *If I need time to think before responding, I ask for time to gather my thoughts to present/address their concerns as needed (and in writing, if necessary).*

Recognizing Beliefs that Cause Problems in Relationships

Just as relationships can be affected by differences in definitions, Individuals and couples can also get stuck when they don't share what they think, how they feel, or if they don't listen to each other fully. Awareness is the key. The following are some common beliefs that I learned through a conference by **David Burns, MD**. I have listed the most common beliefs below that I have observed most often, when working with couples. These beliefs can interfere with couples expressing feelings, listening, and treating each other with respect. Reviewing them will help identify stumbling blocks in your own communication

Beliefs that Commonly Block Expression of Thoughts and Needs:

It's too painful to admit I'm part of the problem.

I can't say how I feel because you are upset.

I will punish you with silence and maintain my innocence.

You should know what I want/feel without me telling you.

Conflict is dangerous.　　I must always try to please others.

I shouldn't feel angry or upset.　　I've tried everything, nothing works.

Beliefs that Commonly Block Listening:

I'm right. You are wrong. This is your fault.

I must argue and defend myself.

I'm not causing the problem. I'm the victim

I'm entitled to better treatment.

One of us must win and one of us must lose.

I don't want to get hurt again.

I will keep you at a distance.

You should think, feel and behave the way I expect.

Beliefs that Commonly Block Respect:

I don't want to be respectful.

They will never change.

I have the right to get even.

I'm too angry.

It won't do any good.

Why should I treat them well?

Notes

Overcoming the Past

Two simple affirmations that can help us heal from the past and leave it behind us, are:

"I forgive and let it go!   That was then, and this is now!"

<u>Anger</u> is often the culprit of the past. We might be angry about hurtful things that have been said or done. Or we might be angry about important things that were not said or were not done.

Anger in and of itself is not bad. It really is a signal of disappointment or an unmet expectation. According to Paul Hegstrom, in his "Learning to Live - Learning to Love" class, anger is a secondary emotion; meaning it's precipitated by another emotion such as: sadness, embarrassment, frustration or fear.

Anger becomes problematic when it gets out of hand or when we fail to acknowledge our feelings. It's okay to become angry. God gets angry. Jesus got angry when he threw the money changers out from the temple of prayer. God's word says to be angry and sin not.

<u>Forgiveness</u> is a way we can deal with anger - anger at ourselves and anger at others. It's important to acknowledge our feelings so we can deal with things in a healthy manner rather than let it eat at us and cause sickness in body and relationships. Telling ourselves the truth about ourselves, others, or a situation, can help let go of anger and forgive.

First, forgiveness is a choice. It usually doesn't happen without us choosing to do so. What does forgiveness mean? Does it mean allowing someone to hurt us over and over? No, forgiveness is an attitude. Forgiveness can be given without agreeing for the hurt to continue to happen. Dixie Carter, from Paul Hegstrom's "Learning to Live - Learning to Love" class, helped me to understand forgiveness as a loving attitude with limits. Forgiveness sets our self and the other person free emotionally. The Bible tells us to love our neighbor as our self; **not** <u>more than</u> our self.

Since then, I have thought about forgiveness and how God forgives. God always forgives when we ask. However, he expects us to be truly sorry for what we did or did not do. He also expects us to change our behavior and attitude. *Then we should not feel bad when <u>we</u> expect acknowledgement of and changes in behavior or attitudes from others either.* It is okay to have expectations. Set limits and establish guidelines to follow. It makes things clear, so everyone knows the rules. It helps to play fair, so the involved persons can enjoy the game, so to speak.

How to forgive when it keeps hurting?

Set limits and reward good behavior only!

Restitution can help with forgiving, as well as acceptance/appreciation of forgiveness when someone continues the undesired behavior after they know it is problematic.

It's okay to ask for repayment when damages have occurred, so learning takes place and behavior stops. It is also okay to ask for some type of restitution, when damages are severe, or someone has broken the law. This is many times necessary, because the person had no regard of the law or for their fellow being. The restitution will help in teaching correct behavior and in serving justice.

Occasionally, one may need to end a toxic relationship. It's okay. We don't have to be close to everyone. We are just supposed to love them like we love ourselves. If we are hurting ourselves in our attempt to love them, we are unbalanced. This is not God's will. Love is a choice and so is forgiveness. They are gifts. Make every attempt to get along and cooperate with others whenever possible. Do what you can. When you cannot cooperate, say No and pray for them.

Apologies can help with forgiveness. _Although, if an apology is given in a way the other person does not value, it may only make things worse!_

How do I forgive my spouse (or someone else)?

1. Pray for them each day. Ask God to help and bless them.
2. Write down what you are having trouble forgiving them for, specifically. Include something you need them to say or do that helps you to forgive them.
3. Ask your spouse to read your writing. Thank them for taking the time to read it as you give it to them.
4. If they do not respond to your writing in a reasonable time frame, ask them to tell you in their own words why you were upset and how you were feeling.

Knowing your spouse (or the other person understands) how you were feeling, will help you to forgive. Also, knowing how they felt at the time and why, will help too. Acknowledge how they must have been feeling. This will help them forgive you.

*Remember, until they learn otherwise, your spouse (or other person) will tend to apologize in the way they value (because they are trying to love you the way they know how); which might be very *different from the way you apologize. The motive is the same however! Both people usually want to repair and have a better relationship. Just because it's not done in the way you want it, doesn't mean it isn't sincere.*

What to do when I have hurt, offended, or neglected my spouse?

Here are some examples of things to say:

1. **"You have put up with this for far too long!"**
2. **"I don't blame you for being upset!"**
3. **"I understand how you would feel _____!"**
   (Be sure to acknowledge the feeling.)

   You can lovingly look in their eyes, hold their hand, hug or give them some space and stay nearby and be accepting. You might take a break and let the apology soak in. ***There is usually one person in the relationship that needs longer time to process and feel the apology.***

Importantly, you can apologize in the way they value. Acknowledge how they must have been feeling. You might ask how you can make it up to them and then do your best to follow through. **You can use the Relationship map at the end of this book to learn what kind and method of apology your spouse values**. This should ensure an effective apology and acceptance of your apology.

I learned this after 20 years of marriage and working with many couples. I learned that typically one spouse values a simple "I'm sorry" rather than an "I'm sorry and an explanation; while the other spouse values an explanation with the "I'm sorry. Both well-meaning individuals may offend the other – purely because they don't value the way it is done. *** *(**Ask your spouse what sincere apologies look, and sound like to them. Then, when you apologize to them, apologize in <u>that</u> way.** *** Things will go much smoother!

*Consider presenting apologies via writing, in addition to verbally. This will allow for re-reading and processing time.

Simple Communication Strategies

1. Communication 1,2,3,4

My most challenging couples have helped me develop a simple communication formula to follow; especially when communicating difficult issues and emotions. This formula helps couples to keep from fighting unfairly. It is the following: (It may require several exchanges before having full closure.)

1. *I feel* _____.*"*
2. *"I like, or I don't like, when* _____.*"*
3. *"I need or want* _____.*"*
4. *"Would you be willing to* _____?*"*

That's it! Keep it simple. ****If a person doesn't like talking about their feelings, they can use steps 2-4. If a person does not like stating what they need, use steps 1, 2 and 4.**

Examples of this formula are as follows:

> I feel afraid.   I don't like when you talk to your old boyfriend. I need assurance.
> Would you be willing to stop talking to him and show me your phone to prove it?

> I feel guilty. I don't like frustrating you.
> I need to be better at communicating my needs with you.

> I feel encouraged.
> I like when you touch my back when sitting on the couch watching TV.
> I need to feel your touches like that. Would you be willing to do that more often?

2. I'm Thinking You are Thinking…

Another simple formula I discovered, can be used for initiating conversation and gently addressing issues you think may be of concern, is what I call the I'm Thinking, You're Feeling Game. (Competitive Couples especially enjoy it.) This formula also helps reduce unfair fighting.

"I'm wondering if you're thinking _____. *Is that what you're thinking?" Or,* *"I'm thinking you are feeling* _____ *about* _____. *Is that how you are feeling?" Or," I'm thinking you need* _____. *Is that what you need?"*

Communication of Weightier Issues or When a Difficult History Exists

The following format will help communicate more weighty issues between couples or individuals within families. It is not necessary to complete every blank on the form – only the ones that apply. Circle the words that apply, as well. A feeling word list is at the bottom.

I have felt _____ for _____.

I'm feeling _____ because _____.

I'm thinking you have been feeling _____ with _____

Because _____. I know you love me because _____.

It really helped/bothered me when _____because, I have

felt/needed _____ when this happens. I'm sorry for _____.

 Will you please forgive me for _____?

I'm willing to _____ and to _____ in the future.

From now on, I will do my best to _____ by _____.

A way you could help me (if/when you can/want) is to: _____,

    when you see/hear/feel me _____.

I want/need you to understand _____. I forgive you for _____.

I want/need you to _____. I understand you need me to _____.

Today I want to _____with/for you. Would you be willing to _____?

Feeling Word Examples: **angry, aggressive, agonized, annoyed, anxious, apologetic, arrogant, attacked, bashful, betrayed, bored, bound, cautious, confident, conflicted, curious, defensive, determined, devastated, disappointed, disgusted, ecstatic, envious, exasperated, exhausted, frightened, frustrated, grieved, guilty, happy, helpless, hopeful, horrified, hurt, indifferent, innocent, interested, irritated, jealous, lonely, mischievous, miserable, misunderstood, negative, obstinate, optimistic, overwhelmed, pained, panicky, paranoid, perplexed, puzzled, regretful, relieved, sad, satisfied, shocked, speechless, surprised, stupid, suspicious, sympathetic, thoughtful, trapped, undecided, unsure, withdrawn, wonderful.**

Communicating Suppressed Feelings

Sometimes it's easier to communicate via writing instead of verbally. This is the case when anxiety or defensiveness is an issue. Often, I suggest to couples/families that tend to fight easily, or who don't typically communicate or communicate in healthy ways, to communicate via a writing journal; which they can keep in a mutually agreed on convenient location.

I feel _____ because _____.

I like when you: _____.

I like when: _____.

For example:

I feel sad because we don't talk much. I feel hesitant telling you this because I don't want to hurt your feelings or be rejected.

I have felt left out and unloved because you seem too busy for me.

I like when you call me on the phone to ask how I am doing. I like when we do things together like going out for coffee. I like being with you because you are special to me.

Further communication can be:

When you see/feel/hear me _____ you can help by _____.

Example: When I seem crabby, you can help by asking me if there is something I need.

When Responding to Communication

I (understand/think) you have been feeling _____, (because/when) _____. I understand you would like me to _____ when _____.

I would like for you to _____ when you (see/hear/feel) me _____ because _____.

For Example: I understand you have been feeling left out. I think you are jealous of the time I spend with your sister. I understand you would like to have a closer relationship with me. I would like that too. When you are feeling left out, I would like for you to tell me. I'm sorry I have not spent time with you when you have asked. Asking me ahead of time will help me arrange my schedule. I will make efforts for a closer relationship in the future because you are important to me and I love you.

Things to Remember when Dealing with Each Other in Difficult Discussions

1. Think the best of each other.

2. Acknowledge your part in the situation.

3. Have an accepting attitude.

4. Agree with each other as much as possible (You can agree to disagree.)

5. Accept the other person as they are.

6. Ask specific questions to make things clear.

7. Ask for what you want and need.

8. Ask how you can make things right/what you can do to make things better.

9. Reward each other for efforts, in a way each person likes.

10. Remember: You are learning! The more you practice, the better you get at it.

11. Remember: You are responsible for your own feelings, words and actions.

12. Instead of being offended, you can ask yourself; is there any validity in what they said?

(The Bible says the wise overlook an insult, and that we all sin.)

It might help deal with feelings by thinking "what is the other person feeling and why would they say that?" This can help put things in to proper perspective. Maybe they are hurt or not feeling well. Or they might just have a different perspective than us, or they present things differently. We can choose to think "It's ok." Regardless, when an insult occurs, it's like paying attention to a thermostat. Someone is not comfortable. We can choose to ask the other person how they are feeling and what they need. If we listen to them first, they will probably listen to us next. It is then that we can start negotiating a situation that is relatively comfortable for both of us. If we choose to get mad and respond badly, things may get worse.

When the other person says how they feel. It's important to name the feeling yourself, such as; "*Oh, you are feeling* _____." It may also help to comment on the feeling, such as; "I can understand how you would feel _____. Or "I want to understand, please tell more."

Notes

Communicating with a Less-Communicative Individual

1) If you want to know what the person really thinks and how they really feel, **learn to ask them what they think or how they feel about something <u>prior</u> to you telling them what you think or how you feel.** (Otherwise, they might not want to disagree with your thoughts or they may feel like you are imposing your thoughts or feelings on them.) **Note:** *Often, they will say "I don't know," just before they come up with an answer. Wait for the answer. The "I don't know" is their step - in thinking and processing.*

2) **When you ask a question, try using the same type of wording they use when they ask you a question.**

3) **You might consider giving them a heads up on what you'd like to discuss and ask when a good time is for them to discuss it.** Individuals avoid communication usually because they need communication prep time to think about the same issue you have been thinking about for a long time. They usually don't want to be taken off guard and they may value accurate and less wording. They want to have well thought out responses.

4) **You might ask them to write their thoughts/concerns out for you to respond better.**

5) **If they seem mad at you, you might ask them if they are mad at you and ask them what you said or did that hurt them. When you ask, ask in a way that says, "I want to hear it and I'm sorry."** Be patient and wait! Offer that they can write it down if it's easier for them to do so.

   Assure them you will be patient and non-judgmental. Phrases like, "It's ok," will help them communicate with you.

   Tell them you need to know how they really feel, because if you do not know, you cannot change your own behavior to ways that work better for them.

   Tell them when you do not know how they feel, you don't feel connected and you cannot satisfy them or make mutually satisfying decisions together.

   Reassure them they are terrific, and you are grateful for them, even if they may say something that is hard for you to hear or say something you don't agree with. (Many times, the reason why the other person doesn't talk is, they don't want to make the other person feel bad or make the relationship worse.) *Tell the other person it's harder on you when you don't know how they really feel.*

6) **After they do talk, be sure to be responsible for your own actions and behavior.**

7) **If it's your spouse, you might want to meet your spouse's need for physical contact, prior to talking.** (It's easier for men to connect emotionally when there is physical contact. The physical connection helps men feel emotionally safer to share thoughts and feelings.) **You might also explain to him that when he clams up** (rarely talks, gives one-word answers, doesn't talk much, or give feedback on the things you say), **you feel the same feelings as he might feel when/if you refused to be intimate with him.**

8) **Explain to them the more the topic is avoided, the greater anxiety you have and the greater and more frequent your need to talk about it becomes. Therefore, it will save both of you time and trouble to go ahead and discuss it.**

9) **Tell them they don't have to have all the answers.** Guys typically feel pressure to know all the answers. When they don't know how to do something you ask, or don't know how to address a problem, they can get crabby and avoid.

10) **If you want the other person to talk more, try spending more time with them while being quiet. Wait patiently. See if they talk more.**

11) **When you ask a question and want more information, simply ask, "More details, please."**

12) **You can invite them to switch roles with you and interact how you interact with them.** This should be an insightful exercise for both of you. The person that does not talk much values quietness. They may see wordiness as annoying.

13) **Say little and choose your words carefully.** They may say more, and your relationship will probably become better connected and more enjoyable.

14) **Thank the other person when they talk to/with you!** Be patient with each other as you make changes over time.

Notes

Communicating Feedback without Hurting Feelings

The following technique I learned from my friend Theresa. She learned it through some training at work. It has three simple steps.

The Sandwich Technique – *Build a sandwich.*

1. **Say something nice about the person.** (It's the bread.)
2. **Tell them what you need or like and why.** (It's the meat or sandwich filling.)
3. **Say something nice again and thank them for listening/caring.** (It's the bread.)

Don't worry so much. They may appreciate your courage and honesty and love you more.

Sandwich Example 1

1. I love you. You care about me.
2. I like when you compliment me. It makes me feel valued by you.
3. Thank you for listening to what I need, and thanks for loving me.

Sandwich Example 2

1. You are important to me.
2. I will enjoy our time together more when we can discuss more things I care about; Like asking me about how I am doing and what I enjoy and talking about some funny experiences you have had and sharing about things other than just politics or people.
3. I hope you understand, and I look forward to getting together again soon, because I value you and our time together.

Family Communications – Dinners and Holidays

The example used in the Sandwich technique section of this book may need to be used prior to family dinners; especially with individuals who seem to hold discussions that annoy others - especially at holiday times.

I have found it helpful to be prepared with discussion questions or stories to share when meeting with family members that haven't been seen in a while. I have recently discovered, through the help of a client, that Madras Gras napkins have conversation questions/thoughts on them which help families connect and communicate in fun and meaningful ways.

It is also helpful to take care of any unfinished interpersonal issues in private, prior to attending family functions, whenever possible.

Quick Reference Communication Tips and Phrases

<u>**For Women to Use with Men**</u>

"I love and respect you."

"Do you mind if _____?"

"Where and what's the plan?"   "More details, please."

"I would like to help. What would be most helpful to you?"

"When is a good time for us to discuss _____?"

"What do you think I'm feeling?"

Would you be willing to _____?

*Remember, the more direct you are, the easier it is for a man to respond. Think slow and steady. Be purposeful and say one thing at a time and keep things simple. Remember it helps them not to get overwhelmed and helps them to respond better.

Quick Reference Communication Tips and Phrases

For Men to Use with Women

"I love you."

"I understand what you are saying. You are saying _____."

> *(This will save you from having to listen to things many times over. It will also help them feel how important they are to you.)*

"It sounds like, or seems like, you are feeling _____." "Tell me more."

"Is there something you need me to do?"

"I don't blame you," or "Explain more" or "I can see how that would be upsetting."

"I'm feeling overwhelmed."

"I know you will figure it out."

Remember, Women are feeling oriented and need to know they have been listened to and their feelings understood.

Team Building /Negotiating   Chapter IV

Sharing Power and Control

<u>Many couples struggle with power and control</u>. **The Bible instructs us in Ephesians 5: 21-25 for us to submit to one another in reverence for Christ. And for wives to submit unto their own husbands, as unto the Lord. For the husband is the head of the wife.** It also instructs **Husbands to love their wives, even as Christ loved the Church, and gave himself for it.**

If we view marriage as a team, in which the Husband is the Coach and the Wife is the Assistant Coach, *it might make things easier to comprehend and help us keep scripture in proper perspective and balance.*

For example: Although a Coach has final decision-making authority, an effective Coach will rely on an Assistant Coach's knowledge and listen to their Assistant Coach's concerns prior to making major decisions. Likewise, an effective Assistant Coach will support the decisions of the Coach and respect the Coach as the leader. Problems happen in marriages when the Assistant tries to be the Coach or when the Coach doesn't take the lead or when the Coach is not listening to the needs and concerns of the team. ***It is much easier for the Assistant Coach to respect and follow the Coach's lead - when she feels listened to.***

It is also easier if both individuals view the playbook each day. Keeping the Bible on the kitchen table makes it easy to consult and read the team play book. A daily scripture reading and prayer at a meal time, helps couples get along and work together as a team.

Further, in Emerson Eggerich's, book <u>Love and Respect</u>, (a good read for couples feeling unloved and disrespected.) he says **men value respect more than love and women value love more than respect. *Because of this, a man will have difficulty doing something his wife tells him to do; especially if it's said or done in a way he perceives as disrespectful and controlling.***

I have found that women may do/say something they themselves perceive as loving, such as helping a man find a parking spot. Most generally, men perceive this as disrespectful and controlling; since they are perfectly capable of finding their own parking spot.

Likewise, a man may not open a woman's car door, because he is trying to show respect in that she is perfectly capable of opening her own door. However, a woman may perceive it as unloving at certain times.

So, it depends on each person and what they perceive as respectful or loving and depends on if it's a man or a woman. In the love/respect section of my "Relationship Map" on pages 80-81, couples can find out what each person views as loving and respectful. It helps take the hurt and fight out of everyday situations.

Team Recipe for Handling Finances

Finances are often an issue among couples; especially when there are limited resources or one of them as a spending problem. Spending issues can sometimes indicate bi-polar disorder. Once it is adequately treated, usually with a mood stabilizer, decision making abilities usually improve and spending is normalized. Life then can be much smoother.

Because money can be a dividing force for many couples, I usually recommend to most couples that they have mutual checking and savings accounts to pay mutual bills and save for the team. This eliminates fighting over who is paying for what. I also recommend each person to have their own additional separate savings account; in which the same percentage of each of their own income goes into it. This way, they each have access to a portion of money that they do not have to have the other person's approval to spend. It is nice to have it to use when there is something one person may want, which is something the other may not agree to, or to use when one wants to surprise the other with a gift of some kind. For Spouses who work at home and raise the kids, I suggest they get the same percentage from the household income as the money earning spouse does, to put in their saving account.

This might seem like an impossible task at times; especially when resources are limited. A small percentage such as 2%-5% of the household income can add up and give each spouse some much needed independence and freedom – even if it only allows splurging on their favorite kind of coffee for the week.

I have found the spiritual practice of tithing, or giving, 10% of the household income to the church or to help others is a practice that ends up helping the overall financial situation. It has helped me to not worry as much about finances either. It seems although it may be a sacrifice to give it at times, the better the financial situation seems to be in general. *If both individuals do not agree in tithing, do not let this be a source of contention.* Instead consider the following options:

1.) Tithe 10% on the income of the person who feels strongly about tithing.

2.) Tithe 10% to others and 10% to the spouse who does not support giving 10% of the household income to others. Once I started giving my spouse 10% of my income each week for him to use as he likes; he agreed and felt good about tithing 10% of his income. This way he felt he had some return for the hard work he does to support the family and he can spend money on his car hobby without feeling guilty.

The other advice I have for handling finances, is for the person that is better at money management, be the one to pay the bills. If both individuals are capable, the one who can handle stress associated with money the best, should be the one to make sure the bills are paid. If neither person is good at money management, consider a trusted person to be a payee. Whoever pays the monthly bills, will want to keep the other person informed of the current financial situation by sharing bill amounts and bank balances with the other. This helps to make sure both individuals understand, trust, and work together as a team. It eliminates the tendency to fighting about finances.

Dave Ramsey is a respected author on managing finances and getting out of debt. Two of his books are called, The Total Money Makeover and Financial Peace. He has also written a book for kids called Smart Money, Smart Kids.

Team Recipe for Disciplining Children

Children are a wonderful thing, yet they can really stress out a marriage. This is especially true when there are step kids involved. **Dr. Matthew A. Johnson** has a method for dealing with discipline fairly and consistently regardless of which kid it is or, who's kid it is. It helps the parents stay of the same team and eliminates fighting due to differing parenting styles.

His method is called "Family Rules." You can learn more by reading his book <u>Positive Parenting with a Plan: Family Rules Book</u> at www.family-rules.com.

My brief explanation/rendition of <u>his</u> method is the following:

1. Parents write out the rules for the family to be posted and read/understood by all. (I.e. no hitting or swearing etc.) Every rule on the list is to be agreed upon by both parents. If both parents in the household cannot agree to the rule, it doesn't go on the list.

2. Parents also write out 30-50 recipe cards, containing (1) 5-15-minute (age appropriate) activity on it. For example: Dust the living room, practice tying your shoes, collect and take out the trash, clean the litter box, read a book to your brother, rub a family member's back, do 10 jumping jacks, clean the toilet, vacuum the living room, etc.

3. Parents also write "Grace" (with a heart) on 5 recipe cards, to add to the other activity cards and assemble, in a shuffled order, in a recipe card box. This box will be accessed by family members each time a rule is broken.

4. When a member breaks a rule, members are to immediately pull a card from the front of the box, read it, and do the activity the card displays on it; whether it's in word or picture form. Cards are to be returned to the back of the box. If a "Grace" card is drawn, no activity is required.

5. Keep a Motivation Jar with things like money, candy, pieces of paper that have activities on them, to choose from when a day or week goes by in which someone has not had to pull a card.

This method's purpose is to get the persons attention off doing the undesired activities and on to doing more appropriate activities. If family members like pulling and doing cards, that is okay. It will keep them from doing undesired behavior and will keep the house cleaner.

This method keeps parents from having to constantly figure out discipline choices, especially during times in which they are busy or stressed. It keeps discipline consistent and in balance. It keeps discipline fair among all family members and avoids issues with jealousy and resentment. It keeps parents from judging each other and/or arguing about discipline. It's easy to implement and ensures that discipline happens and happens in a non-abusive way. It's a brilliant idea because it is a win/win solution to a historically major dilemma.

Team Recipe for Chore Distribution

Another issue of struggle for families involves chore distribution. Dishes and Laundry are the major concerns because of the daily volume and repetitive nature of them. The person responsible for these tasks often becomes overloaded, burdened, and resentful when it is their sole responsibility to do them; especially when they have a job outside of the home.

Since everyone produces, I suggest all members of the family take part in doing the tasks. Not only will it help with family relationships, but it will also help members become responsible/ functioning adults when they have their own houses/families to manage.

Of course, it depends on the number of people in the family. Each person should be responsible for some part of doing laundry and dishes daily. Children as young as 2 or 3 should be able to help get laundry to the basket and their dish to the dishwasher. This is how I suggest tasks are divided up.

Dishes

It is helpful for all family members to pick up their own dishes after eating and take to the dishwasher. In addition to this, each person can be assigned a responsibility based on interest and skill level. Larger families can have one person put condiments in the refrigerator, another person wipe off the table and the counters, another person wash the pots and the pans, while another sweeps the floor, and another takes out the trash.

Making a habit of one person always emptying the dishwasher each morning and perhaps the same person starting the dishwasher every night, allows family members an empty dishwasher each day to add dishes to, as they are dirtied, during the day.

It is also helpful to making a habit of emptying the kitchen trash every night when starting the dishwasher. It makes it more convenient to throw trash away the next day without it piling up.

Chore Distribution Continued

Laundry

Over the years, I have found it easiest to manage laundry when a habit is made for someone in the family to start a load of laundry each morning. If another family member makes a habit of changing the loads when they come home from school or work, it is very helpful. Folding laundry can be done when a member or members watch a favorite TV show in the evening. Each person can be responsible for collecting their pile of things, taking them to their rooms and putting them away at night. If you have members of your family who do not like putting away their clothes and you have one person who likes it and is good at it, that can be their job. Each family member should be responsible for getting laundry to the designated laundry collection site daily.

*When dishes or laundry or any other tasks seem overwhelming and out of control, I have found it best to start with the easiest task and then follow with the next, easiest task. It helps to gain momentum. For instance, the easiest task may begin with throwing a Kleenex away. **Looking for the easiest and most doable thing and then doing it, will help to get the job done; rather than focusing on the mountain of work.***

Phrases that Create an Environment of Cooperation and Teamwork

"**Do you mind if** _____?" and

"**Would you be willing to** _____?"

"**I value your contribution.**" Or, "**Thank you so much for,** _____!"

The above phrases work like magic in cooperation and teamwork with men especially; because they perceive them as respectful. Women, children and teenagers like them too.

Using words like please, although it's polite, can make the other person feel as though they should comply or like they have little choice in the matter.

You will tend to get more honest answers to your questions and greater cooperation with the above phrases.

Affirmations that help with Teamwork and Negotiations:

1. **We work together as a team.**
2. **We create win/win solutions**

Negotiation Strategies

When negotiating, it's important to negotiate at a time that works for both or all involved persons. Negotiating time can be established by asking the question: "When is a good time for you to discuss _____?"

At the agreed upon time, it's important to keep the question "How can we both (or all) get what we want."

When negotiating; identifying the problems, listing concerns, establishing goals and brainstorming solutions are essential. These can be done via discussion or via writing. When topics are especially "hot," writing may be the preferred method.

An example of using this to address a societal issue is:

What are the problems with Immigration?

1.

2.

3.

What are your feelings and concerns about immigration?

1.

2.

3.

What are your goals regarding immigration?

1.

2.

3.

My ideas for addressing immigration are:

1.

2.

Key things to keep in mind when negotiating:

1. Take care of any other unfinished business of the past, if possible, prior to negotiations. This helps with cooperation and fosters positive attitudes.
2. Keep in mind the question, "How can both/all get something we want/need?"
3. Agree whenever possible.
4. Give credit to someone when they have a good idea.
5. It is important to remember each person is different and will look at things differently. To expect 100% agreement is unrealistic.
6. Remember to not be offended if the other person doesn't embrace your first solution.
7. Trading: "Will you do X for me, if I do X for you?"
8. 70%-80% satisfaction goal; in which, unless both/all parties are not 70%-80% satisfied with the outcome, the deal is not equitable, and another solution is sought. In polar-opposite situations, neither person will be 100% happy with the outcome. However, if both are relatively and equally happy with the outcome (at least 70-80% happy with it) it's a win/win solution.

Phrases to use when negotiating may include phrases such as: *It bothers me when _____," "Is it ok if I get _____, in exchange for _____."*

Examples of Negotiated Agreements:

Situation: Bill hates cleaning the bathroom and Nancy cleans bathrooms for a living. Nancy would like a break from cleaning the bathroom at home.

Negotiated Solution: Bill happily cleans the bathroom 1-2 times a month at home in exchange for Nancy to mix up and bake the cookies Bill buys at the store.

Situation: Joe has had a history of being treated poorly by certain members of Cathy's family. Cathy wants Joe to attend important family functions like holiday gatherings, birthdays, etc.

Negotiated Solution: Whenever there is a family event, Joe and Cathy drive separately. Joe congratulates the person being celebrated and talks with family who treat him well. He leaves after a brief appearance to go help a friend in need, of which he honestly arranges prior to each event. This way Cathy is not left to make up some excuse as to why Joe leaves family functions early. Cathy is happy he is involved, and Joe is happy he doesn't have to be in uncomfortable situations in which he has no control. Joe looks like the good guy he is to family members because he showed up and is helpful to his friends.

Situation: Carol and Larry love to entertain. They have two young children. Carol loves to plan, and Larry loves to plan and execute. Both enjoy family time with their own parents. Carol does not like spending time with Larry's Mom because Larry's Mom does not like her and is often rude to her in front of others. Because of this, Carol feels her mother-in-law ruins every holiday and birthday with her family. They do not want to celebrate a birthday more than once or a holiday more than once with family members.

Negotiated Solution: Birthday Parties for the children are celebrated at their own roomy house where they can make food and decorate as they want. Birthday guests alternate each year between Larry's Parents and Carol's Parents. The year in which Larry's parents come to the birthday of the oldest child, Carol's Parents will come to the birthday of the youngest child on the same year. The next year it will be flipped. Since both Larry and Carol like, planning parties, Larry plans the parties for those celebrated with his parents and Carol plans the parties for those celebrated with her parents. Since it is so difficult for both to get time off from work, holiday time must be scheduled way in advance. Holiday gatherings will be alternated between her family and his. If one family visits for Christmas this year, the other family visits for Christmas the following year. This solution ensures fairness and equality in time spent with the Grandchildren, gives them more control, less confusion, and allows both equality in planning gatherings. Larry agreed to help execute the parties Carol plans, for decreasing her stress and give her opportunities to spend time with her family when they visit. Likewise, Carol will help execute Larry's plans when his family visits. This gives her the opportunity to stay busy and not have to interact as much with Larry's Mom. They both can shine and have their own desires met when their own families visit, enjoy their families, and not fight after the event.

Win/Win solutions and satisfaction increase when priorities and values/needs are clear and are accepted in a spirit of love and cooperation. The following section of this book discusses identifying these for more happy and peaceful relationships. My Relationship Map provides a way to identify individual and family needs and priorities.

Relationship Mapping for Peace and Happiness   Chapter V

Love Languages and Priorities

When it comes to healthy/happy relationships, it's important to first know about Love Languages and their significance. Gary Chapman is responsible for coming up with the concept of the 5 love languages including: Words of Affirmation, Physical Touch, Acts of Service, Quality Time, and Gifts. His premise is that we tend to love others in the ways we ourselves like to be loved, if it is not the way the other person prefers to be loved, they won't feel the love to the degree that we are trying to express it.

Speaking another's love language reduces fighting and solidifies the relationship; making it stronger than ever and helps with healing. We have learned to treat others the way we want to be treated. Therefore, we most generally try to love others in the way we deem important. But if it's not the way them deem important, we miss the mark.

When we learn to love others the way they truly value and need, then we truly love them. Love is a choice. As we choose to love others in the way they can understand and connect with, it is then that we are truly doing unto others as we would have them do unto us. Who doesn't want to be loved in a way that is meaningful?

Following is a tool I developed to help you identify what kinds of verbal, physical, service, time, and gifts, are important in the daily lives of those you love. It is based on Gary Chapman's discovery of the 5 love languages. I have added my own discovery of words of acknowledgement, words of connection, and use of endearing terminology to his "words of affirmation" work; along with the frequency of such desired. I have created what I call the "Relationship Map."

It seems like relationships are like putting a 1000-piece puzzle together without seeing the puzzle box. Each person has an image of the perfect or desired relationship in their head. Often, the image is not communicated adequately to the other person. Imagine putting a 1000-piece puzzle together, without seeing the box. It can be done. However, it would take longer and may be very frustrating. That's why I created the "Relationship Map." *It can assist any two people (spouses, parent-child, siblings, or friends) to get along better!*

Although the following "Relationship Map" tool assesses day to day living preferences, it is fun to take the Love Language Evaluations created by Gary Chapman. They can be found in his books: The 5 Love Languages for Couples and 5 love Languages for Children.

Relationship Map for Peace and Happiness - Love Language Needs

The first section of the following Relationship Map is based on Gary Chapman's 5 Love Languages. I created it to assist any two people in identifying daily values/priorities.

Types of Words I Value Most (Circle preferences and frequency desired.)
Words of Acknowledgement: i.e. *"You worked hard on _____."*
Frequency Desired: Daily, Weekly, Monthly, Holidays (verbal /or written?) Other: _____

Words of Praise: i.e. *"You look amazing." "You smell good." "You're good at _____."*
Frequency Desired: Daily, Weekly, Monthly, Holidays (verbal /or written?) Other: _____

Words of Connection: i.e. *"I like when you ____." "I like how you ____." "I love you."*
"I want you to _____." "I want to do _____ with you."
Frequency Desired: Daily, Weekly, Monthly, Holidays (verbal /or written?) Other: _____

Endearing Terms: When you call me Sweetie, Honey, etc.
Frequency Desired: Daily, Weekly, Monthly, Holidays (verbal /or written) Other: _____

Types of Touch I Value Most (Circle preferences and frequency desired.)
Kisses, Hugs, Sitting Close, Holding Hands (Daily, Bi-Weekly, Weekly, Monthly)
Back Rubs, Foot Rubs, Touches on Knee, Shoulder, Etc. (Daily, Bi-Weekly, Weekly, Monthly)
Wrestling, Tickling (Daily, Bi-Weekly, Weekly, Monthly)

Types of Acts of Service I Value **Most** (Circle preferences and frequency desired.)
Keeping Things Picked Up, Dishes, Trash (Daily, Bi-Weekly, Weekly, Bi-Monthly, Monthly)
Laundry, Clean Bathroom, Vacuum, Dust (Daily, Bi-Weekly, Weekly, Bi-Monthly, Monthly)
Lawn Care, Vehicle Care, House Projects (Bi-Weekly, Weekly, Bi-Monthly, Monthly)
Appointment Scheduling, Planning Dates, etc. (Weekly, Bi-Monthly, Monthly, Quarterly)

Types of Time Spent Together I Value Most (Circle preferences and frequency desired.)
Talking, Praying, Dining, Coffee/Snacking (Daily, 2-3 times a week, Weekly)
Walking, Exercising, Resting, Watching TV (Daily, 2-3 times a week, Weekly)
Shopping, Traveling, Movie/Play (Bi-Weekly, Weekly, Bi-Monthly, Monthly)
Dancing, Hunting/Fishing, Racing, Sporting Events (Weekly, Bi-Monthly, Monthly, Quarterly)

Types of Gifts I Value Most (Circle preferences and frequency desired.)
Wrapped /or Unwrapped? Expensive /or Inexpensive? Hand-made /or Store Bought?
Food, Flowers, Jewelry, Clothes, Car Parts, Tools, Sporting Gear, Magazines, Candy,
Vehicle, Trip, Other: _____ (Daily, Weekly, Bi-Monthly, Monthly, Quarterly, Holidays, Yearly)

Relationship Map – Relationship Values

Another thing I discovered about relationships and love Languages is; it's very important to apologize and thank others in ways they value. For Example: My Husband values a simple I'm sorry. I value more words. Two very sincere people may offend each other by the way they attempt to apologize. Sometimes when you give an explanation to a person who values a simple "I'm sorry," they may think you are blaming them or making excuses for your behavior. It will not be viewed as sincere. Likewise, when a person who values apologies with explanation, (etc.) is simply told "I'm sorry," they may get ticked off. The first thought might be, "Does he even know what he is saying he is sorry to?" This can be exasperating and cause more hurt. It's imperative to know what the other person values as a sincere apology. The apology may be taken more sincerely if you pair the apology with a primary or secondary love language of the person you are apologizing to. For example: My Husband might prefer a simple I'm sorry with a gift, at the same time, since his main love language is gifts. For me, it would be best to give me a hug and say I love you with an apology (for example, since two of my main love languages are words and physical touch. Since knowing these things are important, I've included them in my "Relationship Map."

What I Value

Apologies that include: (Circle preference/s.)

"I'm Sorry."   *"I shouldn't have _____."* *"I didn't mean to _____.*

"I'm sorry you're hurting."   *"How can I make it up to you?"*

"I was thinking _____ and I was feeling _____."   *"In the future, I will _____."*

Other: _____

Some people like to prioritize their selections by numbering the preferences they circled, in the order they prefer them in.

Acknowledgement and acceptance of apologies are equally important as apologies.

Acknowledgement/Acceptance of Apologies that include: (Circle preference/s & prioritize.)

___ *"I forgive you."*   ___ *"No Worries!"*   ___ *"Thank You!"*

___ *I believe you."*   ___ *"It's Okay."*   ___ *"I know you didn't mean to _____."*
Other: _____

Relationship Map – Relationship Values

*People like what they like and usually don't deviate. Even if the other person does not do it the way you like, if you can identify that they are doing things the way they like. You can recognize they are trying to love you the best they know how. This reduces fighting and increases levels of satisfaction.

Below you can identify what you value with a "Thank you!"

A **"Thank you"** that includes: (Circle preference/s and prioritize.)

_____ *A smile*   _____ *A hug*   _____ *A kiss*   _____ *A Touch*

_____ *A gift*   _____ *An act of service*   _____ *A "Thank you! I really appreciate it."*

Other _____

*In addition to Apologies/Acceptance of Apologies and Gratitude, it's important to know what kind of greeting the people you love value. If the greeting you give them is not valued, it sets the stage for the following time together to spark discontentment and argument.

The **Kind of Greetings** I Value include: (Circle preferences and prioritize.)

_____ *A smile*   _____ *A Hug*   _____ *A Kiss*   _____ *"Hi!"*

_____ *"How are you?"*   _____ *"Hi Beautiful" (Handsome)*

Other: _____

I must say, it's not imperative the other person does everything the way we like all the time. The purpose of the Relationship Map is to make it clear to the other person what we like. If we are not clear, and they are not clear with us, the less likely we are to know what kind of things the other person needs/wants. Knowing this information allows both to interact in more satisfying ways. Most generally, husbands do try their best to please their wives whenever possible. It's just we wives can be so hard to figure out and know how to please; and vice versa.

Relationship Map – Relationship Values

Another Part of the "Relationship Map" that is helpful for Individuals in all relationships is that of identifying what kind of relationships the other person values.

What I Value Most in Relationships: (Circle preferences and prioritize.)

___ Honesty

___ Gentleness

___ Understanding

___ Direct Communication

___ Being There/Involved

___ Humorous

___ Competitive

___ Financial Stability

___ Practical Help

___ Emotionally Supportive

___ Polite (please, excuse me, thank you and bless you)

___ Appreciative

___ Quiet

___ Adventuresome

___ Surprising

___ Listening with Feedback

___ Lots of Togetherness

___ Independence

Relationship Map – Support and Environmental Needs

*Knowing who or what a person's support system is, will give further insight into what a person needs and values. For example, a support system may look like this:

My Support System and Why (Example)

Mom – She is understanding and a good listener.

Husband – Provides for me, calms me, fixes things, challenges me, and spends time w/ me.

Dogs – Are happy to see me, are always there and are accepting and cuddly.

Daughter – Challenges me to think, makes me laugh, and is fun to talk with.

Dad – Encourages me, helps me practically, and keeps me connected to the world.

My Sister – Helps me practically and has positive attitude.

Mother-In-Law – Makes food and blesses us

My Support System and why: (follow above example)

_____ - _____

_____ - _____

_____ - _____

_____ - _____

_____ - _____

Daily Needs and challenges are also important to identify.

Hours of Sleep I need each night or day: _____ hours

I operate best in these kinds of environments: (Circle preferences and prioritize.)

___ Quiet   ___ Noisy   ___ Chaotic   ___ Organized   ___ Dark

___ Clean   ___ Messy   ___ Relaxed   ___ Musical   ___ Bright

Relationship Map – Struggles and Dreams

Things I find to be difficult: (This will give the other person clues as to how to be helpful.)

Examples: house work, short term memory, sleeping, standing all day, fixing dinner when tired

_____   _____

_____   _____

Things I do that I don't really enjoy: (This will give clues on what to help the other person with/or give insight into the sacrifices they make and what to acknowledge/thank them for.)

_____   _____

_____   _____

Things I really enjoy doing by myself /or with others.

_____   _____

_____   _____

Things I dream about doing:

_____   _____

_____   _____

What I want from life:

_____   _____

_____   _____

What I want to learn:

_____   _____

Places I want to go:

_____   _____

_____   _____

Relationship Map – Communication Timing and Intimacy Needs

*This page is intended for couples and their need to connect through communication and physical intimacy. If the needs of both individuals are not met, on a give and take basis, the marriage will suffer. Love is a choice. Knowing what each other needs is critical.

The best time for me to discuss things: (Circle preferences and specifics.)

Time: Morning   Lunch Time   After Work   Supper/Dinner   Bed Time

Day: Any Day   M-F   Weekend   Days off from work

Specifications: _____

Examples: I would like you to arrange a special discussion time, prior to issues of significance.

I would appreciate knowing what you want to discuss ahead of time (day, 2 days, a week.)

It is ok to talk with me anytime about anything.

You can talk with me at designated times about anything without prior notice.

I will say if I need time to think about something.

I would like for you to discuss heavier issues with me via writing to simplify and expedite

The best time for me to be intimate: (Circle preferences and specifics.)

Time: Any Time   Morning   After Lunch   After Work   After Evening Meal   Bed Time

Day: Any   Monday   Tuesday   Wednesday   Thursday   Friday   Saturday   Sunday

     Days of no work   Other Specifications: _____

(For Intimate Relationships only) The Way/s I Prefer to be Approached when the Other Person Wants to be Close or Intimate: (Circle preference/s and prioritize.)

___*Say you love me.*   ___ *Kiss my neck.*   ___ *Touch my back.*

___ *Grab my body.*   ___ *Give me a passionate kiss.*   ___ *Follow me around.*

___*Ask me if I want to fool around.*   ___ *Ask me to make love with you.*

___ *Ask me to join you on the couch or in bed.*   ___ *Take my hand.*

___ *Ask me to do something with you.*   ___ *Rub my back or shoulders.*

___ *Help me finish what I am doing.*   ___ *Send me a "Love text."*

     Other: _____

Relationship Map – Emotional Response Needs

*Unmet expectations can cause much hurt and conflict when we are not aware of what a person really needs in various situations. As stated before, *people like what they like*, and don't typically deviate from their preference. When preferences are identified, the other person can be smarter in how they choose to respond to the other in various situations. It's like having an owner's manual for your car. Knowing what to do and how to operate safely is valuable with others, in many cases. It should decrease fighting and increase satisfaction when the information is followed. ***It will be helpful to add any specifics, from the Relationship Map, to your phone for easy reference. It is especially important for information that does not come natural to you - as we often pair ourselves with people opposite from us.**

These are Ways I Prefer Others to Respond When I Look or Sound:

Sad/Disappointed or Am Crying: (Circle preference/s and prioritize.)

___ *Hug me.*   ___ *Tell me, "It will be okay."*   ___ *Stay close by me.*

___ *Tell me you understand.*   ___ *Tell me you love me.*   ___ *Don't touch me.*

___ *Hold my hand.*   ___ *Touch my shoulder.*   ___ *Ask if there is something I need.*

___ *Ask if you can help me with something.*   ___ *Tell me I will figure it out.*

___ *Tell me you don't blame me for being upset.*   ___ *Tell me we can talk later.*

___ *Go away and give me some time - _____ minutes.*   ___ *Say nothing!*

Anxious/Overwhelmed: (Circle preference/s and prioritize)

___ *Tell me it will be okay.*   ___ *Ask if there is something you can do for me.*

___ *Get out of my way and do something helpful.*   ___ *Pray for or with me.*

___ *Tell me you understand.*   ___ *Tell me you are here for me.*

___ *Remind me to do Kegels or breathing exercises.*   ___ *Give me a hug.*

Other: _____

Relationship Map Continued – Emotional Response Needs

Crabby/Complaining/Frustrated: (Circle preference/s and prioritize.)

___ Hug me.   ___ *Tell me, "It will be okay."*   ___ *Stay close by me.*

___ *Tell me you understand.*   ___ *Tell me you love me.*   ___ *Don't touch me.*

___ *Hold my hand.*   ___ *Touch my shoulder.*   ___ *Ask if there is something I need.*

___ *Ask if you can help me with something.*   ___ *Tell me I will figure it out.*

___ *Tell me you don't blame me for being upset.*   ___ *Tell me we can talk later.*

___ *Go away and give me some time -* _____ *minutes.*   ___ *Say nothing!*

Other: _____

Happy/Excited: (Circle preference/s and prioritize.)

___ *Say, "I'm glad you are enjoying your day/activity or Say, "It's nice to see you smile."*

___ *Hug me or hold my hand.*   ___ *Celebrate with me.*

___ *Touch my shoulder or kiss me.*   ___ *Tell me you love me.*

___ *Tell me you like when I'm happy and you understand why I am happy.*

Other: _____

Relationship Map – Emotional Response Needs

Angry: (Circle preference/s and prioritize.)

___ *Tell me, "It will be okay."*   ___ *Stay close by me.*   ___ *Tell me you understand.*

___ *Tell me you love me.*   ___ *Don't touch me.*   ___ *Hold my hand.*

___ *Touch my shoulder.*   ___ *Ask if there is something I need.*

___ *Ask if you can help me with something.*   ___ *Tell me we can talk later.*

___ *Tell me you don't blame me for being upset.*   ___ *Tell me I will figure it out.*

___ *Go away and give me some time -* _____ *minutes.*   ___ *Say nothing!*

Other: _____

(For Non-Intimate Relationships) How I like Others to Approach Me when the Other Person wants to be Close. (Circle preference/s and prioritize.)

___ *Hug me.*   ___ *Text me.*   ___ *Ask me to do something with you.*

___ *Sit by me.*   ___ *Give me something to eat.*   ___ *Follow me around.*

___ *Rub my back or shoulders.*   ___ *Tickle me.*   ___ *Take my hand.*

___ *Poke me.*   ___ *Wrestle me.*

___ *Call me on the phone and ask how I am doing.*

Other: _____

The following and final section of my Relationship Map includes a section on discovering what each person feels is most respectful or loving. It is found on the next page. These can be major points of contention when we don't understand the perspective of the other.

These Kinds of Things Show Me Love/Respect the Most (Check or circle preference/s.)

___ Calling me by an endearing name in <u>public</u> / Calling me by <u>my name</u> in <u>public</u>

___ Calling me by an endearing name in <u>private</u> / Calling me by <u>my name</u> in <u>private</u>

___ <u>Not</u> contradicting or correcting me in <u>public</u> / <u>Not</u> contradicting or correcting me in <u>private</u>

___ Making decisions for me / <u>Not</u> making decisions for me / Giving me 2 things to choose from

___ Opening the car door/doors for me

___ Giving me directions; like where to park (for example)

___ <u>Not</u> telling me what to do; like where to park (for example)

___ Listening to me, by restating what I said in your own words

___ Listening to me, by cooperating with what I said and doing it

___ Asking how you can help, rather than telling me what to do

___ Waiting until I am finished with something, rather than interrupting me

___ Letting me lead, when we are doing something together

___ Leading me, when we are doing something together

___ Asking questions when we are doing things together

___ <u>Not</u> asking questions when we are doing things together

___ Supporting my interests and decisions, by asking me about them

___ Supporting my interests and decisions, by accepting them without question

These Kinds of Things Show Me Love/Respect the Most (Check or circle preference/s.)

___ Asking me what I <u>feel</u> about things / Asking me what I <u>think</u> about things

___ Asking me if "I'm sure" of something, if you think something is not right

___ <u>Not</u> asking me if "I'm sure" of something; instead stating your concern directly

___ Being gentle with my feelings / Being direct and stating what you need

___ Stating what you observe and asking what I need, if something seems amiss

___ Stating what you observe and asking what my plans are, when something seems amiss

___ Showing interest in me, by planning dates and family activities I would enjoy

___ Showing interest in me, by planning dates and by planning family activities we can all enjoy

___ Asking me if I want to do X, when, you want to do X

___ Telling me you want to do something, and then ask me if I will join you

Relationship Map Warning: Now that it is clear to both of you what the other needs/desires/expects in a happy relationship, there is the chance you may become bored. If this is the case, resist any temptation to ditch the other person/relationship. Instead, enjoy the peace you have and spice up life together by doing activities to help others, or by going on trips, etc. You will now be more of a blessing to each other and those around you!

Besides the "Relationship Map," there are Relationship Secrets and tips I have discovered from 25 years of marriage and from working with many couples.

Relationship Secrets

Secret 1

One person in a couple usually just wants a simple "I'm sorry."
The other person usually wants an explanation with their apology.

When the person that likes explanations apologizes to the person that sees explanations as not accepting responsibility, it irritates and hurts the other person and comes across as insincere. It ends up doing the opposite of the intention.

When the person who doesn't like explanations just says, "I'm sorry," the person who likes explanations thinks they are just saying it to get the other person to shut up or that they are just saying it because the other person is upset.

The person they are apologizing to does not believe or think the other person fully understands or knows what was even so upsetting. They can get hurt and more frustrated. Therefore, the "I'm sorry" does not have the impact that the person saying it may have meant.

And it goes on and on.

It's helpful when both people recognize and discuss what kind of apologies they value. Give the other person the kind of apology _they_ value. It will save you tons of time and heartache in the future.

Secret 2

When a husband refuses to engage in conversation with his spouse, the rejection she feels is the same to her as the rejection he feels if she would refuse to make love physically with him.

Since conversation is foreplay for women. The satisfaction a husband feels when he physically satisfies his wife, is like the desire and satisfaction she has for communication and meeting her man's emotional needs and vice versa.

It takes both people to move out of their comfort zone and choose to love the other in the way the other needs loved.

Intimacy Relationship Secrets Continued

Secret 3

Women need to feel loved and cherished as worthwhile and "smart."

The secret is: in general, your man already values you as worthwhile and smart. Otherwise, he would not be with you. He just hasn't told you that. It often doesn't seem that way when you have seen their looks of confusion and shakes of the head. Truth is, they just do not understand. Admitting so might make them look not so smart. They have the need to be loved and cherished as worthwhile and smart individuals too.

Men: *Compliment the woman you love. Let her know you appreciate her. Tell her when you Believe she has a good idea about something.*

Secret 4

Besides needing respect, men need to be admired physically.

The secrets are: Men need to be acknowledged not only for the way they provide for their spouse, but also for how well they satisfy them. Sh... They need to have their intimate aspect admired.

Wives: *Be sure to compliment his body, as well as his ability to satisfy and provide for you.*

Secret 5

The spouse that doesn't talk much values the spoken word and quiet. They may view wordiness as annoying. Sh... They also often say "I don't know," before saying something, "Important." *Wait patiently.*

Try just being with the other person. Go where they are. Stay quiet and speak sparingly with choice wording. Be patient. Ask simple phrases like: What do you think about _____? Keep your thoughts to yourself, until later or until asked. When you would like to hear more from the other person when they say something, try a simple phrase like: *"More details, please?"*

The less you say, the more they may say, and the better your relationship may become.

Intimacy Relationship Secrets Continued

Secret 6

"Would You Want To ..." has a different meaning to men than women.

To Men: "Would you want to..." really means, "I really want to ... and I really want you to agree.

To Women: "Would you want to...?" simply means, "Do you have interested in....?"

Not knowing this, can cause a man to get upset and feel rejected by a woman when she does not realize how important the question is. I think this secret exists because men are more casual when they ask women to do certain things. They tend not to say when they really want to do something, unlike women that tend to say when they really want to do something. Likewise, if a woman asks a man if they want to do something (instead of, "if they have any interest in doing something"), a man might do it even though they really don't want to and then be unhappy about it; when it really didn't matter to the woman, because she was just wanting to know if he had interest in it.

* This may not be a difference in gender, but perhaps a difference in communication styles between more communicative and less communicative individuals. However, I have seen commonalities in gender within my counseling sessions with clients.

Secret 7

Women can feel lonelier when a man is at home and watching TV or playing video games than she does when he is not around.

The secret is: Women get offended when not communicated with when their man is around. Men often do not realize this, since they are often happy and content to be around the one they love without talking. It is not the same for women.

Men: Talk to her when the commercial is on or ask what she would like to watch on TV. Do your best to watch something on TV you both will enjoy, or take turns watching each other's favorite show. Invite her to play a video game with you or take breaks from gaming to let her know you love and care about her and what she is doing.

Communication for Intimacy

Communication Phrases for Intimacy

I like when you call me _____.

I like when you _____.

I like when I _____.

I like when we _____.

I like how you _____.

I like when you tell me I _____.

I like when you tell me you _____.

I want you to _____.

I want you to know, I _____.

Traffic Light Communication Method for Intimacy

A common frustration couples have in relation to intimacy, is determining when to pursue or not pursue the other. A couple I worked with gave me the idea for having a communication system based on a traffic light. Now, when she goes to bed she can put a green shirt, yellow sweater or red scarf on the door. This communicates what kind of mood she is in for intimacy that night. The green shirt is the green light, if he is in the mood to proceed. He knows he should proceed with caution when there is a yellow sweater. He knows to respect her space when he sees the red scarf on the door. This solution is helpful in keeping hurt feelings at bay. So often men have told me things would be much easier if he knew what kind of mood she was in. There are times in a relationship when roles (or needs) may be reversed and it may be helpful for the other partner to communicate in this way.

Approaching Intimacy

The relationship map in this book has a section about identifying how individuals within a couple relationship, like to be approached when the other is in the mood to be intimate. I learned something from a female client when she used the analogy of getting into a pool as an explanation of the difference between her and her husband, in approaching intimate matters. It is brilliant! She explained her husband likes to dive right in, while she likes to dip her toes in first and take her time getting use to the water - before she gets in.

Pool Imagery for Intimacy

This information has helped me to assist other clients in better meeting their partners intimacy needs. **Often, men tend to begin intimacy the same way. They often get into a pool by diving or jumping in.** Women tend to approach intimacy and the water more gingerly by getting their toes wet and getting use to the water much more slowly. If the one person is not aware of what the other person likes, the approach to intimacy can either be frustrating or offensive. Imagine one person pushing the other person into the deep end of a pool – not always fun for both!

Since women's brains hook all things together, opposed to men who can think about one subject at a time, it takes women a longer time to process their feelings and get their head in the game, so to speak, prior to intimacy. This can be very frustrating for a man who is "ready" when a woman wants to talk about many things first. Because of this, I suggest each couple have a designated talk time out of the bedroom (earlier in the day or evening). Talk times should be at a time when both individuals are functioning relatively well. When talk time is had daily, it leaves intimate time more sacred and successful.

Communication via writing for Intimacy

Because each person is unique and has unique needs, **I encourage couples (who have issues in the bedroom especially) to have a discussion or write down specifics for each other. Specifics can include how they like to be approached, with the method and order preferred for things to be done, (including types of touches, kisses, phrases etc.) with an approximate timing schedule.** *Men, especially take great pride in pleasing their woman sexually. Knowing exactly what she likes, can allow great success and satisfaction and give room for surprises along the way. Not knowing a key piece of information, may be a hindrance to exceptional love making.*

An example of writing in specifics is as follows: When I ask for a back massage I like my back to be rubbed between my shoulder blades in a large circular motion, with medium pressure, and lasting a minimum of 30 seconds.

Using specifics, as in the back-massage example, makes it clear as to what each person likes. Therefore, each spouse can successfully meet the need or request of the other. It takes the guess work and "hit or miss" nature, out of it.   *Please keep private information out of reach of children.*

Likes and Dislikes in Times of Intimacy

Don't be afraid to say when there is something you don't like. I have found if you include statements of what you do like, with something you don't like, it will be received better by the other person. An example of this is: "I really don't care much for when you _____, but I really like when you _____!"

Intimacy Logistics

Bedtime - *I suggest couples go to the same bed at relatively the same time every night together* (preferably around the time when the person needing to go to bed the earliest gets in bed); *even when not sleeping in the same bed through the night (for health reasons such as snoring or back issues, temperature differences etc.).* ***This allows for important snuggling and intimacy.*** *In cases in which there is differing shift work or sleep schedules, etc.; that person can get out of bed and go take care of what they need to - after spending time together in bed.*

TV in the Bedroom

I also find it necessary to talk about TV. Since it is a huge distraction and can interfere with quality sleep (because of the blue light that awakes the brain) and can be the same as dumping garbage into your subconscious mind if it is on during sleep (because your conscious mind is not able to filter the information). ***I recommend there to be <u>NO</u> TV in the bedroom unless it is on only during designated times in which both individuals are awake.*** In situations in which a person cannot fall asleep without noise, I recommend soft instrumental music or sounds without words. This allows your subconscious mind to rest, so you can function at your best.

Cell Phones in the Bedroom

Remember to switch cell phones to *"Night Mode"* prior to bed. Blue light emissions tend to wake the brain and interfere with sleep. Keeping cell phone/facetime use limited to mutually designated times earlier in the evening, will ensure marital harmony and quality sleep.

Children and Intimacy

I suggest that all couples have a designated date time and alternative date time each week. This allows couples to prepare for intimacy without the worry of children. *Remember to lock the bedroom door, at other times of intimacy, when children may be around.*

Maintaining Happiness and Intimacy   Chapter VII

Keep lines of Communication open. Ask for what you need. Explain why. Discuss daily plans of action. Make sure both or everyone understands and knows what to do.

Sentences like these might be helpful to use during the day: "When is a good time to discuss _____?" "How can we both get what we want?" "Would you be willing to _____?"

Consider presenting requests and apologies via writing, rather than via a verbal exchange. This will allow time to process and respond appropriately.

*When necessary, you can agree to disagree and yet accept/love the other person.

Daily Ways to Wow your Woman

1. **Ask what she thinks/feels about something & have a conversation about it.**
2. **Tell her something you like about her each day.** *"I like how you _____."*
3. **Ask her how you can help her or what you can do to make her life easier and do it.**

Remember these kinds of things
The "I love you!" and "How was your day, dear?"
"Is there anything I need to apologize for?" (When, she seems upset with you.)
"Will you forgive me for _____?" I understand you felt _____"

Tip: When your wife continues over and over about something, try naming her feeling. Saying something like, "It sounds like you are feeling _____," should help her to feel understood and calm down. Then you can redirect (unless she first needs to hear an apology from you) with something like: "Where can I take you for dinner?" Or you might offer to pray with her or help her with something.

Daily Method to Mesmerize your Man

1. **Touch/or flirt with him to let him know he is desired.**
2. **Tell/or show him how much you appreciate/respect his efforts to provide for & "Love" you.**
3. **Ask him if there is something you can do for him to make his life easier or more "Enjoyable," and do it.**
   Guys like to hear "I love you!" too. They also like for their woman to pray for them.

Maintaining Happiness and Intimacy in Your Relationships

Weekly Maintenance

The 1-10 scale (10 being high)

It will help to regularly ask your spouse or anyone else you have a relationship with (a child, parent, or friend), how things are going for them. You can ask how happy they are with the relationship on a scale of 1-10. You can also ask them, "How can I make it a 10?" This will help give you the information you need to attain the relationship goals you desire.

Using the 1-10 scale strategy can also help communicate issues of importance with your partner such as: This issue affects me at the level of a 7 or 8. An example is: If you'd be willing to work less hours each week, my stress level would decrease by a 9. This method can help guys, especially, to get an idea of how serious an issue is. Often, spouses get exasperated with the other when they tell them there is a problem, and things don't change. *Using a number scale to communicate issues, help to make things more concrete and understandable.* This way partners can more accurately assess the damage and adjust as necessary.

Schedule Weekly Date/Alternate Together Time

It is important to spend specially designated time with each other. Having an alternate time, when a babysitter cancels or work calls, helps to ensure your special time together is not compromised. Sundays are often a good time to plan and arrange family and dating schedules.

Weekly Communication Connection

Using the communication sheet found on page 46, can help ensure that important issues are communicated and handled regularly. Couples can use it at weekly date times to expedite clear healthy communication. This leaves more time for enjoying fun activities.

Other Tips for Couples in Maintaining Happiness and Intimacy

1. **For Couples who are Competitive** – *Make a habit of spending time playing a game each day; such as connect four or chess, etc.* Take turns playing each other's favorite game/s. This will help meet your need for competition and keep you from bickering. It helps keep the competition limited to the games and out of the bedroom, so to speak.

2. **For Couples who are Renovating a Living Space** - Remodeling a living space can be very hard on a couple, due to things being disorganized and the financial burden and unexpected costs associated with remodeling.

If you are doing the work yourselves and working together, it's important to **establish a project leader for the day**. The other person will be their assistant.

If both of you want to do the same thing, take turns. *Also, take turns if* neither one of you wants to do something that needs to be done or ask someone else to do it.

*Do together only the things you can agree on together. *It eliminates bickering.

If one of you does not feel safe with the project, **STOP immediately and pay attention! Listen to each other!** Safety is a must!

There may be times you may want to agree to do things independently - when you don't agree on the method. Or you may want to take turns doing it the other person's way. If neither way works well for one or both of you, *try a third (different) way.*

Final Word

*If you are still having major problems in your relationship after reading this book and applying the concepts, remind yourself that you are responsible for your attitudes and behavior only. Remember there could be medical issues that need attention. Seek out professional expertise by seeing a Physician, Psychiatrist, and/or Counselor.

Thank you for reading this book! May God bless you and your relationships!